Endorsements for the Flourish Bible Study Series

"The brilliant and beautiful mix of sound teaching, helpful charts, lists, sidebars, and appealing graphics—as well as insightful questions that get the reader into the text of Scripture—make these studies that women will want to invest time in and will look back on as time well spent."
Nancy Guthrie, Bible teacher; author, *Even Better than Eden*

"My daughter and I love using Flourish Bible Studies for our morning devotions. Lydia Brownback's faithful probing of biblical texts; insightful questions; invitations to engage in personal applications using additional biblical texts and historical contexts; and commitment to upholding the whole counsel of God as it bears on living life as a godly woman have drawn us closer to the Lord and to his word. Brownback never sidesteps hard questions or hard providences, but neither does she appeal to discourses of victimhood or therapy, which are painfully common in the genre of women's Bible studies. I cannot recommend this series highly enough. My daughter and I look forward to working through this whole series together!"
Rosaria Butterfield, Former Professor of English, Syracuse University; author, *The Gospel Comes with a House Key*

"As a women's ministry leader, I am excited about the development of the Flourish Bible Study series, which will not only prayerfully equip women to increase in biblical literacy but also come alongside them to build a systematic and comprehensive framework to become lifelong students of the word of God. This series provides visually engaging studies with accessible content that will not only strengthen the believer but the church as well."
Karen Hodge, Coordinator of Women's Ministries, Presbyterian Church in America; coauthor, *Transformed*

"Lydia Brownback is an experienced Bible teacher who has dedicated her life to ministry roles that help women (and men) grow in Christ. With a wealth of biblical, historical, and theological content, her Flourish Bible Studies are ideal for groups and individuals that are serious about the in-depth study of the word of God."
Phil and Lisa Ryken, President, Wheaton College; and his wife, Lisa

"If you're looking for rich, accessible, and deeply biblical Bible studies, this series is for you! Lydia Brownback leads her readers through different books of the Bible, providing background information, maps, timelines, and questions that probe the text in order to glean understanding and application. She settles us deeply in the context of a book as she highlights God's unfolding plan of redemption and rescue. You will learn, you will delight in God's word, and you will love our good King Jesus even more."
Courtney Doctor, Coordinator of Women's Initiatives, The Gospel Coalition; author, *From Garden to Glory* and *Steadfast*

"Lydia Brownback's Bible study series provides a faithful guide to book after book. You'll find rich insights into context and good questions to help you study and interpret the Bible. Page by page, the studies point you to respond to each passage and to love our great and gracious God. I will recommend the Flourish series for years to come for those looking for a wise, Christ-centered study that leads toward the goal of being transformed by the word."

    Taylor Turkington, Bible teacher; Director, BibleEquipping.org

"Lydia Brownback has a contagious love for the Bible. Not only is she fluent in the best of biblical scholarship in the last generation, but her writing is accessible to the simplest of readers. She has the rare ability of being clear without being reductionistic. I anticipate many women indeed will flourish through her trustworthy guidance in this series."

    David Mathis, Senior Teacher and Executive Editor, desiringGod.org; Pastor, Cities Church, Saint Paul, Minnesota; author, *Habits of Grace*

PHILIPPIANS

Flourish Bible Study Series
By Lydia Brownback

Judges: The Path from Chaos to Kingship

Esther: The Hidden Hand of God

Luke: Good News of Great Joy

Philippians: Living for Christ

1–2 Peter: Living Hope in a Hard World

FLOURISH
BIBLE STUDY

PHILIPPIANS

LIVING FOR CHRIST

LYDIA BROWNBACK

WHEATON, ILLINOIS

Crossway is a publishing ministry of Good News Publishers.

RRDS		32	31	30	29	28	27	26	25	24	23	22
13	12	11	10	9	8	7	6	5	4	3	2	1

With gratitude to God
for
Kathleen Nielson,
who so beautifully models faith, love, and spiritual maturity

"Join in imitating me, and keep your eyes on those who
walk according to the example you have in us."
Philippians 3:17

CONTENTS

THE TIMING
OF PHILIPPIANS

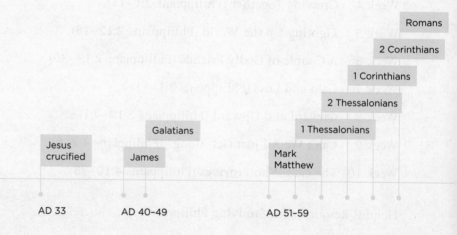

Romans

2 Corinthians

1 Corinthians

2 Thessalonians

1 Thessalonians

Galatians

Jesus
crucified

James

Mark
Matthew

AD 33   AD 40–49   AD 51–59

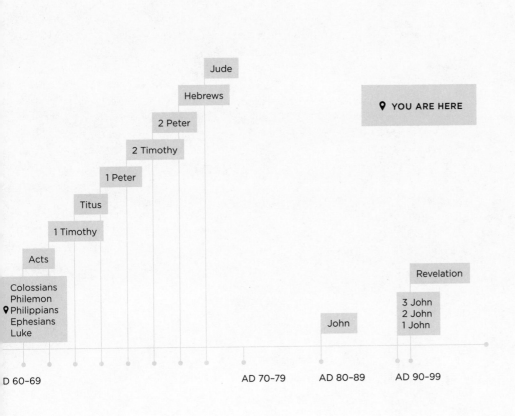

Jude

Hebrews

2 Peter

2 Timothy

1 Peter

Titus

1 Timothy

Acts

Colossians
Philemon
Philippians
Ephesians
Luke

YOU ARE HERE

Revelation

3 John
2 John
1 John

John

D 60-69   AD 70-79   AD 80-89   AD 90-99

INTRODUCTION

GETTING INTO PHILIPPIANS

Hardship, loss, longing, and grief—who among us hasn't experienced some, if not all, of these pains? Those of us who have walked long with the Lord know that following him doesn't shield us from pain. In fact, being his disciple actually intensifies some of our difficulties. The apostle Paul knew this firsthand. Serving Jesus cost him dearly, and he suffered a lot for his faith. As we consider the challenges he faced, we might be a bit puzzled when we first read his letter to the Philippians and notice how often he writes about joy. Paul suffered more than most for the cause of the gospel, yet he was one of the most joyful people the world has ever known. How was this possible? That's what we're going to find out as we study this letter, and we'll learn that the joy he lived is meant for us too. No matter what we're dealing with—past pain, present trouble, or dread of something future—joy is possible. Actually, it's more than possible—it's guaranteed if we've been united to Christ by faith. Through that union, we have the Holy Spirit dwelling in us, and the fruit of the Spirit includes joy. It's true of everyone united to Christ by faith. That being said, our experience of joy is diminished sometimes because we're so easily sidetracked. That's where Paul can help us. The Lord is eager that we find what Paul found and experience the joy he had—not just on one of those exceptionally good days, but all the time, even in painful seasons.

WHO'S WHO IN PHILIPPIANS

Featured most prominently in Philippians is the apostle Paul, the author of the letter. He reveals a good bit about his personal background here, and in this letter he is not shy about expressing his feelings! So we're going to learn a lot *about* Paul as we do our study, but more importantly, we're going to learn *from* him.

The young Timothy, Paul's ministry intern, also has a role in the letter. Timothy was with Paul when the letter was written, and, like Paul, he had lots of affection for the men and women in the Philippian church. This young man Timothy meant a great deal to Paul, as we'll see, and Paul holds

Pronunciation Guide

Philippi: FILL-uh-pie

Epaphroditus:
  e-PAP-fro-DITE-us

Euodia: ewe-oh-DEE-uh

Syntyche: sin-tick-ee

Clement: cle-MINT

out this young man as a powerful example of godliness. Epaphroditus is yet another godly model for Christians to imitate. A member of the Philippian church, he made a risky journey to help Paul and almost died in the process.

Two women come to the forefront late in the letter—Euodia and Syntyche. Sadly, these two are at odds with each other, and, for the good of the whole church, Paul is eager to help them resolve their differences. Of course, when we're considering who's who in Philippians, we must include the believers of the church in Philippi. Although they have no active voice in the letter, we're going to learn a lot from them too.

Finally, and primarily, is God. Undergirding the entire letter is the work of Father, Son, and Holy Spirit.

Philippi in the Time of Paul (c. AD 60)[1]

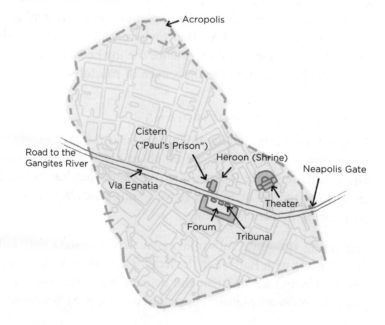

Paul's Second Missionary Journey (Acts 15:36–18:22)[2]
c. AD 49–51

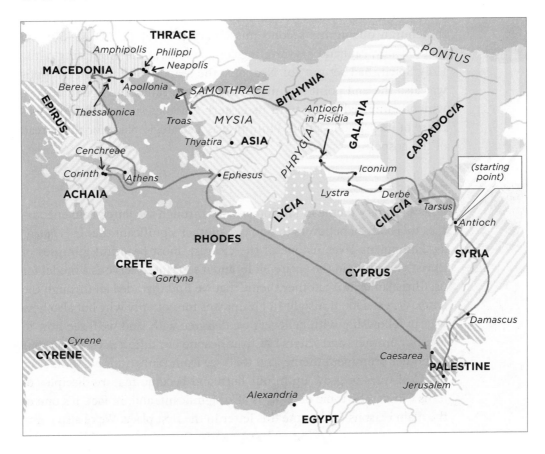

Paul's Second Missionary Journey

Paul's second missionary journey focused on the cities of the Greek provinces of Macedonia and Achaia, including Philippi, Thessalonica, Berea, Athens, and Corinth. This second journey probably began in AD 48 or 49 and ended in 51.[3]

SETTING

Paul's letter was written to the church in the city of Philippi, a strategic colony of Rome, sometime around AD 62. The apostle had established the church during his second missionary journey (c. AD 48–50). On that journey, Paul and his traveling companions, at the prompting of the Holy Spirit, had set out for Neapolis, the seaport of Philippi. Neapolis was also the end point of a major trade route called the Egnatian Way, which connected Rome with its eastern colonies such as Philippi. Because of its prime location, Philippi was a strategic place for the spread of the gospel.

THEMES

Joy is a primary theme in Philippians. All through the letter, Paul encourages this body of believers to rejoice. Another significant theme is *humility*. Philippians gives us one of the clearest, most beautiful glimpses of Christ's humility in the entire Bible, and it's meant to serve as a model for us. Christian *unity* is another theme that we find threaded all through the letter. We get a lot of insight in Philippians for not only why but also how we can fellowship with believers we disagree with, and we'll see how to love our brothers and sisters in Christ despite our differences. *Discipleship* is another prominent theme, and we'll see from Paul's example some very practical ways to grow up in our faith and become mature disciples of Jesus Christ. The topic of *giving* is also significant, and, in fact, it's one of the main reasons Paul wrote this letter in the first place. We're also going to touch on topics of *prayer* and *contentment*. Overarching all these themes is a question for us to consider as we study: *What do we live for?* Nowhere in the letter does Paul actually ask the question, but it comes through in how he describes his reason for living—Jesus Christ. He makes crystal clear that love for Jesus motivates his choices, his desires, his calling, and his relationships. And living for Jesus is why he was joyful and contented no matter his circumstances.

STUDYING PHILIPPIANS

At the beginning of each week's lesson, read the entire passage. And then read it again. If you are studying Philippians with a group, read it once more, aloud, when you gather to discuss the lesson. *Marinating in the Scripture text is the most important part of any Bible study.*

GROUP STUDY

If you are doing this study as part of a group, you'll want to finish each week's lesson before the group meeting. You can work your way through the study questions all in one sitting or by doing a little bit each day. And don't be discouraged if you don't have sufficient time to answer every question. Just do as much as you can, knowing that the more you do, the more you'll learn. No matter how much of the study you are able to complete each week, the group will benefit simply from your presence, so don't skip the gathering if you can't finish! That being said, group time will be most rewarding for every participant if you have done the lesson in advance.

If you are leading the group, you can download the free leader's guide at https://www.lydiabrownback.com/flourish-series.

INDIVIDUAL STUDY

The study is designed to run for ten weeks, but you can set your own pace if you're studying solo. And you can download the free leader's guide (https://www.lydiabrownback.com/flourish-series) if you'd like some guidance along the way.

> *Marinating in the Scripture text is the most important part of any Bible study.*

Reading Plan

	Primary Text	Supplemental Reading
Week 1	Philippians 1:1–11	Acts 16:6–15
Week 2	Philippians 1:12–26	
Week 3	Philippians 1:27–30	Acts 16:16–40
Week 4	Philippians 2:1–11	
Week 5	Philippians 2:12–18	Numbers 15:1–10; 28:1–8
Week 6	Philippians 2:19–30	Genesis 17:9–14
Week 7	Philippians 3:1–11	Acts 9:1–19
Week 8	Philippians 3:12–4:1	
Week 9	Philippians 4:2–9	
Week 10	Philippians 4:10–23	2 Corinthians 11:24–28; 12:7–10

FROM THE FIRST DAY UNTIL NOW

PHILIPPIANS 1:1–11

Someone has wisely observed that if we get to the end of our lives with just two or three friends—those who've been with us through every change, stage, and season—we are rich in friends. Most of our friendships don't survive all those life changes because they are circumstantially based—same neighborhood, same-aged kids, same school or gym. When those commonalities change or end, there's no bond left. It's different with Christian friends though, and that's because the primary thing that bonds us will always remain the same—our union with the Lord Jesus. Have you ever noticed that when you're with other believers, it feels like family? That's actually because it *is* family, and you're more free to be yourself and to share openly about life's ups and downs. Plus when you serve the Lord together, the bond that forms is much greater than the bond forged through sharing a workout routine or a kids' carpool. It's richer, deeper, and eternal. Well, we see this shared affection at the beginning of Paul's letter to the Philippians. It's clear how very much he values—and misses—his Philippian friends. Their mutual affection is so clear because, although their face-to-face time has been limited over the years, they've shared together in Christ and partnered in ministry. That's the background Paul has in mind as he takes up his pen.

1. GRACE AND PEACE TO YOU! (1:1–2)

The apostle Paul, accompanied by his young protégé Timothy, begins his letter to his Christian friends at Philippi with both warmth and humility.

✦ What does Paul convey by designating himself and Timothy as slaves or servants?

....

....

....

....

✦ Paul refers to the believers at Philippi as "saints" (v. 1), which is simply a way of indicating that they belong to Jesus Christ, and he specifically names the church leaders—the overseers (today we're more likely to call them *pastors* or *elders*) and the deacons. According to the passages below, what did these overseers and deacons do and what kind of people were they supposed to be?

· Overseers (Acts 20:28; 1 Timothy 3:1–7; Titus 1:7–9):

Keep watch

Above reproach

blameless; not given to drunkeness

· Deacons (Acts 6:2–3; 1 Timothy 3:8–13):

Worthy of respect, sincere

Uphold the faith

· Based on what you see in these passages, what is the primary difference between overseers and deacons?

tested 1st ~

uphold the faith ~ preach the word

Paul then offers a blessing of grace and peace, which was a standard greeting in those days, even in letters not written by Christians. Back then the word used for *grace* simply meant "greetings," but no doubt Paul used it here in its fuller Christian meaning, which is about our acceptance with God and all the other blessings Jesus won for us in his death on the cross.

✦ The greeting of "grace and peace" appears in other New Testament letters as well (for example, Titus 1:4; 1 Peter 1:2; and 2 Peter 1:2). As you consider this expression, why do you think grace comes before peace?

Grace = undeserved

Overseers and Deacons

The terms *overseer, elder, pastor,* and *shepherd* all refer to the same office. They are called to care for church members, shepherding the spiritual growth of God's people. Deacons are also officers of the church, and the qualifications for deacons are very similar to those for overseers. Deacons, like overseers, are to demonstrate godly character.

---

2. GOSPEL PARTNERSHIP (1:3–8)

This is where we begin to see Paul's great affection for the believers at Philippi, and he is profoundly grateful for their friendship and that they partner with him in ministry.

✦ How in verses 3–5 is Paul's gratitude for the Philippians expressed in his prayers?

Their joy - prayer of partnership

𝄐

Lydia

Lydia was among the women gathered for prayer at the riverbank in Philippi when Paul came to them with the gospel message. She was the very first one to respond in believing faith. Lydia, who had come from the city of Thyatira, sold cloth treated with an expensive purple dye, which was used to make clothes for royalty and other wealthy people. Upon coming to saving faith, she and her household were baptized, and she opened her home as a gathering place for Paul and the other apostles. No mention is made of a husband, so Lydia was likely unmarried, perhaps widowed. Whatever her marital situation, it seems she was well able to provide for those in her home and show generous hospitality to those in the church at Philippi. (Her story is found in Acts 16:11–15).

✦ Paul is so thankful for their partnership, which, he says, was evident "from the first day" (v. 5). On Paul's second missionary journey, he came to the city of Philippi with the good news of the gospel. He'd heard about a place for prayer near a river bank, so one day he went there in hopes of sharing the message of salvation. There he found a group of women who listened to him, and out of this group the church in Philippi was born. Read Acts 16:6–15 and note what stands out to you about the founding of this little church.

Women · God led them thru

Asia → not allow, Kept from

Paul has absolute confidence that God is at work in the lives of his Philippian brothers and sisters, because it's always how the Lord works in his people: "I am sure of this, that he who began a good work in you will bring it to completion at the day of Jesus Christ" (v. 6).

✢ How do the following passages—one from later in this very same letter—shed light on what Paul means by God's "good work" here in verse 6?

· Romans 8:28–30

Sharing Gospel + believers

· Philippians 2:12–13

Keep up the good work you've been doing

✢ Paul's affection for the Philippians is strong because, as fellow believers, they all have a share in God's grace. These believers have stuck with him through all the challenges of his ministry in Philippi and beyond, from the confines of prison to his travels for the gospel. What do we learn from Paul's words in verses 7–8 about the nature of Christian fellowship?

3. PRAYER FOR LOVE (1:9-11)

While Paul no doubt cares deeply about the day-to-day concerns of his friends in Philippi, his prayers for them most often focus on their spiritual needs. Here in verses 9–11, he prays about the quality of their love.

✦ Paul prays in verse 9 not only for flourishing love but for love that's characterized by knowledge and discernment. How do the following passages help us understand the nature of this knowledge and discernment?

Knowledge	Discernment
Proverbs 1:7	Proverbs 17:24
Luke 1:76–77	Romans 12:2
Colossians 2:2–3	1 Corinthians 2:14
2 Peter 1:2–3	Hebrews 5:14

Paul adds in verses 10–11 that knowledge and discernment fuel spiritual growth, a growth theologians call *sanctification*. This is the process by which, over time, we are transformed to resemble more and more our Savior Jesus Christ until that day when he returns to take us home forever—"the day of Christ" (v. 10).

✦ How, according to verse 11, does this "fruit of righteousness" come about in our lives?

....

....

....

....

✦ What is the ultimate purpose for our abounding in love?

....

....

....

....

Love—how we define that word depends on who we talk to, right? For some, love is all about romance and sexual chemistry. For others, to love is to accept alternative lifestyles and pass no judgment on how people choose to live. The Bible's definition of *love* is much richer and deeper than either of these ideas, and sometimes biblical love looks more like hate in the eyes of the world.

✦ We find much more about love in the other New Testament epistles. How do the following passages deepen your understanding of the sort of love Paul prays for the Philippians?

· 1 Corinthians 13:1–13

....

....

....

· Colossians 3:12–14

....

....

....

....

....

· 1 John 2:15–17

....

....

....

....

....

· 1 John 3:16–18

....

....

....

....

....

· 1 John 4:7–21

....

....

....

What do you live for, Lydia?

One who heard us was a woman named Lydia, from the city of Thyatira, a seller of purple goods, who was a worshiper of God. The Lord opened her heart to pay attention to what was said by Paul. And after she was baptized, and her household as well, she urged us, saying, "If you have judged me to be faithful to the Lord, come to my house and stay." And she prevailed upon us.
(Acts 16:14–15)

✤ The abounding love that Paul prays for accompanies spiritual growth, as believers are filled with the "fruit of righteousness" (Philippians 1:11) produced in those united to Christ by faith. How do the following passages illuminate what this fruit is?

· Romans 1:16–17

· Galatians 5:19–23

· James 3:17–18

> "A love which is directed by an enlightened mind
> and a holy heart not only has the capacity to detect
> counterfeits but sweetly realizes the excellence
> of divine things and delights in them."[4]

LET'S TALK

1. Who are your closest friends—and why? Discuss what bonds you together and whether the affection you share is similar to what Paul enjoyed with the Philippians. On the flipside, consider friendships at different points during your life that haven't lasted. If you simply drifted apart, identify what change brought about that drift.

....

....

....

....

....

....

....

2. No doubt we pray for our friends, but how often do we pray like Paul did for the Philippians?

> It is my prayer that your love may abound more and more, with knowledge and all discernment, so that you may approve what is excellent, and so be pure and blameless for the day of Christ, filled with the fruit of righteousness that comes through Jesus Christ, to the glory and praise of God. (1:9–11)

Consider the various components of Paul's prayer for their love and then talk about how this sort of love might play out in concrete ways in your life and through you to the lives of friends and loved ones. How do our prayers for our friends align with Paul's prayer for his friends? Maybe you have a friend in need of discerning love or another who needs the sort of love that stirs up fresh zeal for righteousness. Whatever the particulars, this prayer—in whole or in part—is a good one to pray for every believer we know.

TO LIVE IS CHRIST

PHILIPPIANS 1:12-26

What do you live for? How you answer that question determines everything about your life. What you live for governs your choices big and small. It shapes your passions and the paths you pursue. And it shapes your perspective on life's ups and downs. The apostle Paul's overarching, driving passion—the heartbeat of his entire life—is revealed in this week's lesson. As we learn about what motivated Paul, and what enabled him to respond with joy to horrendously difficult circumstances, we'll grasp more fully what it means to belong to Christ by faith. We'll also learn more about how Christ equips us to handle our circumstances, good and bad, with joy and in a way that brings blessing for ourselves and others. Paul shows us that, in Christ, loss of freedom, unjust treatment, malicious envy, and even the threat of death are actually opportunities.

1. SUFFERING AND THE SPREAD OF THE GOSPEL (VV. 12–18a)

We remember that Paul is writing this letter from a Roman prison to thank the believers in Philippi for sending him practical aid in order to make his days in prison a bit more comfortable. But his primary purpose for writing is simply to encourage these believing friends as they live out their own faith and wrestle with some interpersonal challenges within their church. In this section, Paul tells them about his current situation and how God is powerfully at work through his imprisonment, even when certain people, dominated by envy, try to make trouble for him.

> *"Instead of talking about how he was doing,*
> *Paul talks about how the gospel is doing."*[5]

✦ Paul writes in verse 12 that his imprisonment has actually served to spread the gospel. Where, according to verse 13, has the spread occurred?

....

....

....

....

✦ How do verses 12–13 change our perspective on our own suffering of various kinds?

....

....

....

....

✦ Paul was in prison because of his faith, which inspired other Christians living in Rome to be bold in talking about their own faith (v. 14). In the same way, we might find ourselves motivated to be more bold about the gospel when we read about believers today being persecuted for their faith. Why do you think others' suffering for their faith affects us this way?

....

....

....

....

✢ While Paul's imprisonment inspires some to teach God's word boldly, others take advantage of his situation to teach for selfish purposes. How does Paul contrast the two types of teachers in verses 15–17, and what motivates each type?

	Motivation for Preaching
Godly Preachers	
Selfish Preachers	

✢ Why is Paul able to remain joyful as certain preachers seek to harm him?

✢ What more do we learn from the following passages about what motivates preachers who cause harm?

  · 1 Timothy 6:3–5

· 2 Timothy 3:1–9

· Titus 1:10–11

> *"God continues to advance the gospel through the weakness and suffering of his people today. This does not make that suffering good, . . . but it illustrates that beautifully appointed buildings, large parking lots, and programs designed to attract demanding church shoppers do not guarantee that God is at work. God typically works through means the world rejects."*[6]

2. REASON FOR LIVING (1:18b-26)

Despite some very real troubles—imprisonment and self-centered preachers—Paul's joy is unhindered so long as the spotlight shines on Christ. Paul also rejoices because he is confident that he will be delivered from his difficulties. The word we translate as "deliverance" in verse 19 actually means "saved"—Paul is confident of his salvation, whether or not he is physically delivered from prison.

✦ What do we learn in verse 19 about prayer?

....

....

✦ Paul's confidence rests in the fact that the Holy Spirit is at work in his life, work that he describes in verse 19 as "the help of the Spirit of Jesus Christ." One way or another, the Spirit will deliver Paul from his troubles. What do the following passages add to our understanding of the Spirit at work in Paul—and in believers today as well?

· John 14:15–17, 26

....

....

....

· John 16:7–11

....

....

....

· Romans 8:26–27

....

....

....

✦ Verses 20–21 are the key to understanding the entire epistle and, in fact, to understanding everything about Paul himself. Here we are given the reason for his joy, his courage, his outlook—his whole reason for living. What is this reason?

....

....

....

✦ Paul is torn between conflicting desires in verses 22–26. What does he choose—and why?

....

....

....

....

....

....

....

....

What do you live for, Paul?

"For to me to live is Christ, and to die is gain."
(Philippians 1:21)

✦ What does Paul reveal in verse 23 about what happens to believers at death?

....

....

....

....

Paul is at peace about his own well-being—whether he lives or dies. His concern is focused on his brothers and sisters in Christ, and for their sake, he's confident that the outcome of his imprisonment will most likely be release rather than execution. It's better for his friends if he remains alive.

....

....

....

....

"Christianity is fellowship with Christ."[7]

✦ Through his ministry, Paul wants to cultivate in the Philippians "progress and joy in the faith" (v. 25). Glance back through the letter at what Paul has written so far and then note what you think he means by "progress."

....

....

....

....

LET'S TALK

1. Paul contrasts two types of preachers—those who teach from good will and those who teach from envy and a competitive spirit. When, where, and how might we be tempted to exercise our spiritual gifts for personal advantage? The church is the most logical arena, but consider social media and other platforms that can tempt us to self-promotion. Similarly, how can we guard against envy of someone else's gifts and talents and avoid competing with our sisters in Christ?

....

....

....

....

....

....

2. Paul wrote, "For to me to live is Christ, and to die is gain" (v. 21). Do you share his passion, or does it seem a bit foreign and scary to you? If so, what are you afraid of? If you can't yet relate to Paul's passion, are you willing to pray that the Lord will change your heart so that his lordship determines every choice, every relationship, and every plan you make?

STANDING FIRM

PHILIPPIANS 1:27-30

It matters not only what we believe but also how we live. The choices we make, the passions we indulge, the relationships we form—all these and more demonstrate what we really believe about the gospel. Does our lifestyle reveal that the gospel is life-changing? Do we demonstrate that Jesus is the way to eternal happiness? Unbelievers hear our claims about Christ, but what do they see? What we *do* is as vital as what we *say*. Skeptics see what we do: sacrifice or selfishness, building up or tearing down, spiritual delight or sinful pleasure. It matters how we live. It matters how Christians treat one another. And it matters how we suffer. Paul has been telling his Philippian friends about his priorities and what motivates him to live with such little self-concern. He's made abundantly clear that Jesus Christ is his whole reason for living, and he hopes his own example will be contagious. With that in mind, he begins to instruct the believers at Philippi how to live out of the same mindset he has.

1. UNITED (1:27-28)

Paul begins this section of the letter with a command: "Let your manner of life be worthy of the gospel of Christ" (v. 27). The original Greek words Paul used here had to do with citizenship: "Live as worthy *citizens*." He was likely speaking into a sense of national pride here, which was common for citizens of Rome. The believers in Philippi might enjoy all the privileges of citizenship, but way more important—and far more privileged—is the fact that they're citizens of God's kingdom.

✦ Identify the three aspects of Paul's command in verses 27–28.

1. ....

2. ....

3. ....

....

> *"Christians are to live worthy of their spiritual possessions.*
> *If you are a Christian, you do not hold your possessions*
> *in Christ through any virtue of your own. What you*
> *have you only have from him who is the King of kings.*
> *But having it, you must live worthy of your calling. Old*
> *things are to be put away; all things are to be new."*[8]

✦ We can summarize Paul's instructions in verses 27–28 as a call to unity. Why do you think Christian unity is part of living a life worthy of the gospel?

....

....

....

....

The "opponents" Paul mentions in verse 28 are different from the opponents he identified earlier, in verses 15–17. Those earlier opponents are professing believers who, in their envy, seek to harm Paul and his ministry. Here in this section, the opponents are unbelievers who persecute Christians. Paul shows us that their attacks actually serve a spiritual purpose.

✢ In verse 28 Paul says that the courage of believers in the face of persecution is a "clear sign" of both the persecutors' eternal destruction and the believers' salvation. How do the following passages shed light on what Paul means?

· Matthew 5:10–12

· 2 Thessalonians 1:4–12

2. GRANTED TO YOU (1:29-30)

Paul tells the Philippians that suffering persecution is actually a gift from God, something "granted" to them (v. 29), just as it's been granted to him. Paul holds up his own suffering as both a model for them and an indicator of the ministry partnership they all share, reminding them of the persecution he experienced while he was in Philippi.

✢ What reason does Paul give in verse 29 for why Christians suffer persecution for their faith?

"If you bear a proper witness for Jesus Christ, as God intends you to do, there will be persecution for you."[9]

Read Acts 16:16–40, which recounts the occasion of Paul's suffering for the gospel in Philippi, and answer the following questions.

✦ What did Paul do in Acts 16:16–19 that stirred up anger and got him in trouble?

....

....

....

....

....

....

....

Silas

Silas was a leader in the Jerusalem church. Silas joined Paul as a coworker on his second missionary journey. Silas is also called "Silvanus" in the New Testament letters, and he worked closely with the apostle Peter as well as Paul.

✦ The owners of the slave girl, being residents of Philippi and therefore Roman citizens, had the credentials to make a case against Paul as they dragged him before the authorities. What lie do they tell the magistrate in Acts 16:20–21, and what happens as a result?

....

....

....

....

✦ How does Paul's persecution and suffering serve to advance the gospel in Acts 16:25–34?

....

....

....

....

The next day, the city authorities sought to release Paul from custody, and that's when they discovered that, in their haste the day before, they'd made a huge blunder—Paul himself was a Roman citizen. As such, he was entitled to Roman rights and privileges, one of which was protection from the hasty arrest and type of beating he'd experienced at their hands. When the authorities realized their mistake, they just wanted to be rid of Paul, and they urged him to leave quickly and quietly. Paul refused, however, insisting on a public apology. His insistence had nothing to do with pride but everything to do with the reputation of the gospel. If he were to simply slip away, all the residents of Philippi who'd witnessed his arrest might have assumed he was actually guilty of a crime. Paul's concern there was for the gospel.

✣ That episode in Acts 16:16–40 is likely Paul's earlier "conflict" that the Philippians witnessed and of which he reminds them here in the letter (2:30). How would this reminder encourage the Philippians to have courage as they too experience persecution?

The City of Philippi in Paul's Day

The city of Philippi became a Roman colony in 42 BC. Citizens of Roman colonies enjoyed special status. They were exempt from lots of taxes, and they had more rights when it came to owning land. Philippi in Paul's day was styled after Rome. Citizens worshiped Roman gods, and emulated Roman culture. There was a theater, shops, and even a sports facility. Philippi prospered because of its location along a major trade route between Europe and Asia. For all these reasons, citizens took pride in being Philippians.

What do you live for, Silas?

They seized Paul and Silas and dragged them into the marketplace before the rulers. . . . The crowd joined in attacking them, and the magistrates tore the garments off them and gave orders to beat them with rods. And when they had inflicted many blows upon them, they threw them into prison, ordering the jailer to keep them safely. Having received this order, he put them into the inner prison and fastened their feet in the stocks.

About midnight Paul and Silas were praying and singing hymns to God, and the prisoners were listening to them.

(Acts 16:19, 22–25)

✤ When Paul and Silas were released from prison, they went to the home of Lydia (Acts 16:40). If you recall, she was the first convert in Philippi, and immediately afterward she opened her home to the apostles (Acts 16:13–15). How did Lydia live out in concrete ways Paul's earlier exhortation: "Only let your manner of life be worthy of the gospel of Christ" (1:27)?

....

....

....

....

LET'S TALK

1. Write down five words to describe yourself. How does your list reveal how you see yourself—your personal identity? The Philippians were committed believers, but their identity as Roman citizens was sufficiently important to them that Paul felt the need to remind them of their eternal, lasting citizenship in God's kingdom. Identify people, places, positions, or perspectives on which you might be tempted to build your identity. For some, it's a political viewpoint. For others, it's an experience from the past or a current struggle with sin. For still others, it's a relationship or a job or a ministry role. How can our union with Christ reshape how such things define us?

2. Most of us in the West don't suffer persecution for our faith the way believers in Paul's day did. But some of us do. Even when our lives aren't threatened, we can face scorn, ridicule, and rejection. In a different letter, Paul wrote, "Indeed, all who desire to live a godly life in Christ Jesus will be persecuted" (2 Timothy 3:12). Describe a time when your faith proved costly to you in some form or fashion. Did it make you bolder in willingness to identify with Christ or more timid? Discuss some practical ways to face this fear.

GROWING TOGETHER

PHILIPPIANS 2:1-11

"Look out for number one," right? We're told it's the only way to be happy, the only way to get what we want out of life. But talk to anyone who's adopted that motto, and you'll find cynicism and unhappiness. Putting ourselves first never delivers what it promises, because God didn't design us to live that way. He made us in his very own image, which means we were created to live like Jesus did—sacrificing ourselves to bless others. That's Paul's overarching lesson for us this week. It's a challenge for sure, but he shows us how. And we'll also see why it's necessary for the health of our relationships and for genuine unity. Paul has been urging the believers in Philippi to get along for the sake of the gospel and for their own spiritual growth. He's aware, even from his prison cell, that there's tension in the Philippian church. We know of one specific instance, which we will examine later in our study—two women who don't get along with each other (4:2). Perhaps there were other cases as well. Whatever the particular church dynamics in Philippi, Paul continues to stress the importance of unity. He's going to show us how Jesus Christ is both the how and the why, the source of our unity and the example to follow. And as Paul directs our gaze to Christ, he presents us with one of the fullest, clearest glimpses of Jesus Christ in the whole Bible.

1. LOOKING OUT FOR ONE ANOTHER (2:1-4)

Paul so very much wants his friends in Philippi to get along well that he links his personal joy to their unity.

✢ Paul lists four traits in verse 1 that ought to be evident and thriving among believers. He begins his list with the word *if*—"*If* there is any . . ."—but the word *if* here is meant to imply "since"—"*Since* there is . . ." After all, he knows these believers and what's going on in their fellowship, both the bad and the good. What four traits does Paul list in verse 1?

1. ....

2. ....

3. ....

4. ....

✢ Because those traits are already present in the Philippian believers, they actually are able to live out the type of unity Paul describes in verse 2. According to verse 2, what does unity look like?

....

....

....

....

✢ Look again at the traits listed in verse 1. How do you think that these traits make the unity of verse 2 possible?

....

....

....

....

✢ Describe the contrast Paul sets up in verse 3.

....

....

....

....

✦ Paul certainly isn't saying that we are to think poorly of ourselves or to believe that accepting mistreatment is a mark of godliness. How does verse 4 refine our understanding of Paul's words in verse 3?

....

....

....

....

✦ Read about what Jesus did in John 13:1–17. How does this passage help us understand what Paul is saying here in Philippians 2:3–4?

....

....

....

....

2. EXALTED SERVANT (2:5-11)

To firmly establish his case for unity—Christian unity, which is rooted in humility—Paul holds up Jesus as the be-all and end-all example. He shows us the nature of our Lord and Savior in poetic language. Many see this section as a sort of hymn.

✦ Before Paul begins the "hymn," he tells the Philippians in verse 5 how to approach it. What does he instruct in verse 5, and what does he promise along with the instruction?

....

....

....

....

> *Jesus Christ "is called Son because he is the Son of the Father from all eternity. When he becomes incarnate, he becomes the son of Mary, the promised son of David, the Messiah. But there was never a time when he became the Son of God; that is who he eternally and essentially is. For us and our salvation, the eternal Son became the incarnate Son."*[10]

The content of Paul's teaching here is so rich that we could easily do an entire ten-week Bible study on just verses 6–11. But since we can't do that, we will break it down as best we can.

✤ How is Christ's humility revealed in each of the following verses?

- v. 6

- v. 7

- v. 8

Paul begins by taking us back to the time before Christ became a human being. Theologians call it Christ's "preexistence." He was then and has always been the Son of God, even before he took on human flesh. Plus the Son had the "form" of God then (v. 6), which means that he's always had the exact nature of God the Father and has always been equal to the Father.

Paul goes on to say in verse 7 that Christ, by being born as a man, willingly "emptied himself," but this doesn't mean that he gave away his divine nature. By his own free choice, he set aside the privileges—the power and strength—that are rightly his as God, but he never ceased to be God. He emptied himself by becoming human.

As a man, Jesus obeyed God the Father in his mission—to suffer death on the cross to pay for the sins of God's people. In verse 8 Paul says that Jesus's obedience was an act of humility. Being crucified was a shameful way to die. Victims were raised up on a cross and attached to it with nails or ropes and then left naked and exposed to ridicule and the forces of nature until they died. This prolonged and excruciatingly painful means of execution was reserved for the lowest of the low, the very worst sort of criminals and also slaves. But Jesus was willing to suffer this death for our sake, in our place. He took on the punishment we deserve so we can enjoy his status as beloved Son of the Father.

> *Jesus Christ "is the source of our life, and we must stay close to the source if we are to realize the self-giving life he advocates."*[11]

✦ According to verse 9, what was the outcome of Jesus's humble self-giving?

> *To exalt means "to raise in rank, power, or character and to elevate by praise or in estimation."*[12]

"Jesus" was the name given to the Son of God when he became a human being. "Christ" is the title he was given for his mission on earth, and it comes from the Greek word meaning "anointed one." In the Old Testament Hebrew language, that same title is the word *Messiah*. Paul doesn't tell us here "the name that is above every name," but likely it is the name "Lord." This word reflects God's personal name, which appears in the Old Testament with small capital letters: LORD. Whenever we see Lord written that way, it's the ancient Hebrew name for God—*Yahweh* or "I AM."

✦ Read Exodus 3:13–15, where God reveals to Moses his most special name, Yahweh, which means "I AM WHO I AM." How does this passage in Exodus shed light on why this name fits the exalted Christ?

✦ Placing our trust in Christ for salvation is an act of humility. It's to acknowledge that we can't save ourselves because we are just too sinful. And if we embrace Christ for salvation, we will, from that day on, enjoy spiritual riches, and one day we will share in his joyous exaltation. But those who refuse him—the arrogant in heart—will inevitably be humbled too. According to verses 10–11, how will that happen?

What do you live for, Mary, mother of Jesus?

The angel Gabriel was sent from God to a city of Galilee named Nazareth, to a virgin betrothed to a man whose name was Joseph, of the house of David. And the virgin's name was Mary. And he came to her and said, "Greetings, O favored one, the Lord is with you!" But she was greatly troubled at the saying, and tried to discern what sort of greeting this might be. And the angel said to her, "Do not be afraid, Mary, for you have found favor with God. And behold, you will conceive in your womb and bear a son, and you shall call his name Jesus. He will be great and will be called the Son of the Most High. And the Lord God will give to him the throne of his father David, and he will reign over the house of Jacob forever, and of his kingdom there will be no end."

And Mary said to the angel, "How will this be, since I am a virgin?"

And the angel answered her, "The Holy Spirit will come upon you, and the power of the Most High will overshadow you; therefore the child to be born will be called holy—the Son of God. . . . And Mary said, "Behold, I am the servant of the Lord; let it be to me according to your word." And the angel departed from her.
(Luke 1:26–38)

LET'S TALK

1. Let's admit it—we pause for a moment when we read Paul's words, "Count others more significant than yourselves" (v. 3). And then we might initially feel relief when we get to the next verse: "Let each of you look not only to his own interests, but also to the interests of others." *Whew!* we think. *So I still can look out for my own interests so long as I include others' interests in the process.* Most likely, though, Paul's words about looking out for our own interests are basically an assumption that people quite naturally look

out for their own interests. In other words, he's not calling us to do so! In light of that—the fact that we naturally take care of ourselves—how do we manage it while also prioritizing the interests of others? Discuss what this might look like in particular situations or relationships.

2. Look again at Paul's portrait of Jesus in verses 5–11, a portrait of humble servanthood that we're called to model in our own lives. But we will never follow in his footsteps and serve others if our hearts aren't humble. The problem is that none of us is humble by nature; our humanness makes us naturally proud instead. Discuss how our hearts are made humble. In addition to the example of Jesus in verses 5–11, consider also Deuteronomy 8:1–3; Matthew 18:1–4; James 4:6–10; and 1 Peter 5:5–7.

LIGHTING UP THE WORLD

PHILIPPIANS 2:12-18

Growing up in Christ involves effort. If you've walked with Christ for a while, likely you've realized that growth requires your participation. And there's bound to be failure along the way; sometimes the Christian life seems like two steps forward, one step back. When we're struggling with temptation and find ourselves taking one of those backward steps, a well-meaning friend might tell us, "Just let go and let God," but this isn't going to help us very much because it's not completely true—we have an active part to play in obedience. Another friend might come along and say, "God helps those who help themselves." But this isn't true either—God always helps his children, even when they refuse to help themselves. So what *is* true? We're left wondering if we can make concrete progress in conquering those same old sins that suck us down again and again, or if we'll ever live out the sort of love, joy, and peace we're supposed to have as Christians. Well, this week we're going to see how spiritual growth actually happens. We'll also see some aspects of spiritual maturity that we should prayerfully aim toward, including getting along with our brothers and sisters in Christ. Last week, Paul painted one of the most beautiful word-portraits of Christ in the whole Bible as a way to encourage his Philippian friends toward unity. Now Paul builds on that message as he instructs the Philippians to live out their faith in everyday life. As they grow and mature spiritually, both their joy and their impact for the gospel will increase.

1. WORKING OUT WHAT GOD WORKS IN (2:12-13)

In these two verses Paul instructs his friends to continue their pursuit of spiritual growth, what theologians call "sanctification."

✦ We learn in verse 12 that we play an important role in our spiritual growth. How do the following passages shed light on Paul's instructions to "work out" our salvation?

> • Ephesians 4:10–16

> • Colossians 1:9–10

> • 2 Peter 1:3–8

Sanctification

Sanctification refers to the transforming work of the Holy Spirit in a believer's life, whereby the person becomes increasingly more like Christ. This ongoing process continues until the redeemed person is resurrected and made completely holy in heaven.[13]

It's important that we're clear on what Paul does *not* mean when he tells believers to work out their salvation. First, he most definitely is not saying that we have to earn our way to heaven with good deeds. Christ had to die on a cross because there's absolutely no way we could ever be good enough to get there on our own. We are just too sinful. Even our best deeds are tainted by sin. Second, he is not saying that our lapses into sin and our failures of discipleship will destroy our salvation. Once we've been united to

Christ by faith, nothing we do or fail to do can change our status with God. This is why theologians distinguish between justification and sanctification. *Justification* is a one-time event in which Christ's righteousness is applied to us, thereby securing us eternal life. *Sanctification* is what happens after we've been justified. It's an ongoing process in which we are progressively transformed to be more and more like Christ our Savior. It's that follow-up process, sanctification, that Paul has in mind here.

When Paul explains how we are to work out our salvation—our spiritual growth—he writes that we are to do it with "fear and trembling" (v. 12). He doesn't mean that we should be afraid of making God angry or fear that God is just waiting to punish us if we stumble along the way. Paul's phrase, "fear and trembling," implies respect and awe, which, in turn, are possible only for those who have that humble attitude he showed us in his portrait of Christ in 2:6–11.

✦ According to verse 13, why is spiritual growth, or sanctification, not only possible but actually guaranteed for believers?

✦ How do the following passages help us understand God's role—his working in us to will and to act—in our spiritual growth?

  · Romans 8:26–30

  · 2 Thessalonians 2:16–17

> *"If you have come to God, it is only because God has first entered your life by his Holy Spirit to quicken your will, to open your eyes to his truth, and to draw you irresistibly to himself."*[14]

· 2 Thessalonians 3:3–5

....
....
....

· Hebrews 13:20–21

....
....
....

✦ In Philippians 2:13 what does Paul say is the ultimate reason for why God works in us?

....
....
....
....

2. SHINING LIGHTS (2:14-16)

The world notices. When we claim to trust God, people watch to see if we really do and what trust actually looks like. Are we joyful Christians? Do we express our gratitude for all Jesus has done for us? How do we respond when crises hit or when prayers aren't answered the way we hope? The world notices. They notice when we're joy-filled and peaceful, and they notice when we're anxious about our lives or fretful in difficult circumstances. In all we say and do, we communicate to others whether following Christ is worthwhile—or not.

✦ In verse 14 Paul insists that his believing friends live their lives without grumbling, complaining, or engaging in deliberate controversy. Our words—our conversations—present a significant testimony of what we truly believe about the Lord. Paul also talked about grumbling in his first letter to the Corinthian church. In that letter he reminded believers of what happened to the Israelites centuries before when they'd complained about their circumstances. Take a glance at that story, first the original in Numbers 14:1–12, 29–37 and then the recap in 1 Corinthians 10:1–10. How does that episode in the history of God's people reveal why grumbling words are such a big deal?

✦ As we noted already, Paul's concern here is not just the spiritual growth of his friends but also their witness to a watching world. How, in verse 15, does Paul contrast Christian believers to people in the world?

✦ Jesus also described disciples as lights in the world. In Matthew 5:14–16, what did Jesus say is the outcome of godly living?

✦ In Philippians 2:16 Paul reveals the how-to. What will enable believers to persevere, living so that they reflect the goodness of God and the power of Christ to save?

_____

_____

_____

_____

_____

_____

_____

✦ How do you think we *hold fast* to the word of life (2:16)? You might want to look at Romans 8:2–6 to help you answer.

What do you live for, believers in Philippi?

You Philippians yourselves know that in the beginning of the gospel, when I [Paul] left Macedonia, no church entered into partnership with me in giving and receiving, except you only. Even in Thessalonica you sent me help for my needs once and again.
(Philippians 4:15-16)

_____

_____

_____

_____

Paul has every hope that his investment in the Philippians will stand the test of time, proving on the day when Christ returns that these friends have persevered all the way along the path of discipleship.

3. SACRIFICIAL SERVICE (2:17-18)

Paul has no qualms about doing whatever is necessary to help his friends in Philippi stay strong in their faith, and he communicates his willingness with imagery from an offering that was made as part of the Old Testament regulations governing worship. In making this type of offering, wine was poured either onto the ground or onto an altar along with a sacrifice of an animal or grain. (You can read more about these drink offerings in Numbers 15:1–10 and 28:1–8). The offering was meant to communicate a life "poured out" in God's service. Later, in another letter, just before he was executed, Paul talks about himself using the same "drink offering" language (see 2 Timothy 4:6). Paul's point both times is his willingness to give his life for the sake of the gospel and the salvation of others.

✦ In verses 17 and 18, how does Paul characterize the faith of the Philippians, and what result does he expect from it?

LET'S TALK

1. Consider the process of sanctification, of becoming more Christlike over time. Describe a situation or circumstance in which you were conscious of actively living out Paul's edict in verses 12–13 to work out what God is working in. What was the result? Discuss also how you've experienced sanctification as a process, sometimes a frustratingly slow one!

....

....

2. Paul considers that, by faith, he and his Philippian friends are sacrificial offerings poured out in service to Christ (v. 17). If we find this image shocking, perhaps it's because the call to Christian service is often packaged in much softer, less "extreme" language today. Discuss ways in which you are either pouring your life out for Christ's sake or resisting opportunities to do so. Whichever way you lean at present, what is motivating you?

....

....

....

....

....

....

....

....

A COUPLE OF GODLY FRIENDS

PHILIPPIANS 2:19-30

Every close relationship in our lives leads us to either flourish or diminish—each friend makes us more like Christ or more like the world. That's why it's important to be discerning as we form our closest associations. We do well to consider whether, over time, our various friendships truly inspire us to pursue the Lord more fully and to cultivate our gifts and talents for use in God's service. Of course, the impact of our relationships goes beyond just *us*. Every one of our relationships brings about flourishing or diminishing in the lives of others too. Sure, we want to cultivate godly friends, but we also want to be the sort of friend that others choose. The apostle Paul was an ideal friend for his Philippian brothers and sisters. He encouraged their faith and taught them God's word. Paul had godly friends also, and they helped and encouraged him. This week he identifies two of them—Timothy and Epaphroditus—and he holds them out as the kind of friends we all want to have—and be. What Paul tells us about these two men, his ministry coworkers, shows us qualities to aim for as we seek to grow spiritually.

1. TIMOTHY: NO ONE LIKE HIM (2:19-24)

Timothy was Paul's son in the faith, a young man whose belief Paul had nurtured and watched grow. Over time Timothy had become invaluable to Paul, not only in ministry but also personally.

✦ Read Acts 16:1–3, where we first meet Timothy, and note what you learn about this young man.

....

....

....

....

We're told in Acts that Paul circumcised Timothy. Way back in the first book of the Bible, God set up circumcision as a sign, a mark, of his covenant with Abraham and all Abraham's descendants, who later multiplied and became the nation of Israel. Circumcision was a visible sign that identified a man or boy with the Lord and his people Israel, the Jews. In Timothy's case, because Timothy had a non-Jewish father, he'd never been circumcised. Before Paul would allow Timothy to join him on his missionary travels, Timothy had to undergo this rite because an uncircumcised Jew on the missionary team could have hindered the spread of the gospel among Jews who'd been careful to keep this covenant sign. In order to get why this was such a big deal, you might want to take a few minutes here to read Genesis 17:9–14.

✦ Back now to Philippians 2, why does Paul want to send Timothy to visit the Philippian church?

....

....

....

....

✦ According to Paul here, how does Timothy model the sort of Christlikeness Paul wrote about in 2:3–4?

....

....

....

....

✦ What does Paul reveal in this section about his relationship with Timothy?

✦ How do the following passages—personal remarks from Paul's other letters— enhance our understanding of the relationship Paul and Timothy shared?

· 1 Corinthians 4:16–17

· 1 Thessalonians 3:1–3

· 1 Timothy 1:2–4

· 1 Timothy 1:18–19

2. EPAPHRODITUS: RISK TAKER (2:25–30)

Paul puts before his readers another example of a Christlike life, Epaphroditus, who is well-known to the believers in Philippi.

✦ How does Paul outline the ministry work of Epaphroditus in verse 25?

....

....

....

....

✦ What do we learn about Epaphroditus in verse 26?

....

....

....

....

✦ How does Paul describe the Lord's intervention in Epaphroditus's life in verse 27?

....

....

....

....

"A real mark of Christian maturity is the ability to work with others cooperatively under the banner and for the cause of Jesus Christ."[15]

🔸 Where in this passage, verses 25–30, do we see others-centered love in both Paul and Epaphroditus?

....

....

....

....

....

....

....

🔸 According to Paul in verse 29, how are men such as Epaphroditus to be treated, and why? You might also want to take a look at 1 Corinthians 16:17–18 and 1 Thessalonians 5:12–13 to provide a fuller answer.

....

....

....

....

What do you live for, Timothy?

I hope in the Lord Jesus to send Timothy to you soon . . . I have no one like him, who will be genuinely concerned for your welfare. . . . You know Timothy's proven worth, how as a son with a father he has served with me in the gospel.
(Philippians 2:19–20, 22)

If you recall, one reason for Paul's letter is to thank his Philippian friends for sending him financial support to help him through his imprisonment. But were it not for Epaphroditus's willingness to deliver the gift, Paul might not have received their aid. That's what Paul means in verse 30 when he writes of the risk Epaphroditus took "to complete what was lacking" from the Philippians.

✦ Think about the impact of Timothy and Epaphroditus on Paul and the believers in Philippi. What is it about such men that builds up other believers?

....

....

....

....

LET'S TALK

1. Do you have friends who encourage you and others the way Timothy and Epaphroditus encouraged Paul and the Philippian church? And would others claim you as that sort of friend? Describe such a friend from your own experience. Discuss also what it takes to become a Timothy or an Epaphroditus for others.

....

....

....

....

....

....

....

2. Paul laments a bit that there are so few like Timothy, people who look out for the welfare of others. Instead, he said, "they all seek their own interests, not those of Jesus Christ" (v. 21). Of course we have to practice good stewardship of our lives—our families, our jobs, our homes—so we know that Paul isn't implying in verse 21 that those things don't matter. Discuss what you think he *does* mean and some practical ways to live it

out in our daily lives. Let his words in 2 Timothy 3:1–5—his very last letter—guide your discussion.

_____

_____

_____

_____

_____

_____

_____

_____

GAIN AND LOSS

PHILIPPIANS 3:1–11

Where does your confidence rest? Given that the question is being asked in a Bible study, most likely you know the "right" answer: Jesus Christ. And no doubt your answer is truthful—you do trust in Christ. In reality, though, most of us, without even realizing it, struggle to trust in him—and only him—all the time. When it comes to our well-being, often it's Christ *plus* our health and toned physique, Christ *plus* our husband and kids, Christ *plus* belonging to our particular church denomination. There's nothing wrong with enjoying the good things God gives us. There is a problem, though, when we come to depend on them to give us the good life. When we rely on anything or anyone besides Christ, we find nothing but disappointment and frustration. And if we trust in anything or anyone besides Christ to save us—to make us right with God—it's not just about disappointment; it's a matter of life and death. Being in the "right" church doesn't make us right with God, nor do our good deeds or our Bible knowledge. Being right with God comes only in and through Jesus. This is where we have so much to learn from the apostle Paul. His confidence—for every single thing—rested solely in Jesus Christ. For him, it was Christ plus nothing. But that wasn't always his story. Before knowing Jesus, Paul trusted in himself—his superior background, his good works, his personal righteousness. But he came to realize that seeking security in anything besides Jesus was pointless. So how are we actually saved? Where is our confidence there? That's the big question Paul answers this week.

1. REJOICE, REJOICE, AND REJOICE SOME MORE (3:1)

We've reached a turning point in the letter. "Finally . . . ," Paul begins. (Some of your translations might have "Further . . ." or "In addition . . .") Paul is moving toward his conclusion now, but before he gets there, he wants to emphasize some very important things.

✦ What does Paul instruct in verse 1, and why does he emphasize it so strongly?

....

....

....

....

✦ Paul writes a good bit about joy in this letter, which carries an especially powerful punch since he's in prison. Trace the joy and rejoicing in this letter through the following passages.

　· 1:4–5

....

....

....

　· 1:17–18

....

....

....

　· 1:25

....

....

....

· 2:1–2

· 2:17–18

· 2:28–29

· 3:1

· 4:1

· 4:4

....

....

....

· 4:10

....

....

....

....

*"Happiness is circumstantial, but joy is not. Joy is an
inner quality of delight in God, and it is meant to spring
up within the Christian in a way totally unrelated to the
adversities or circumstantial blessings of this life."*[16]

✛ How do the joy passages threaded throughout the letter shape your understanding of joy?

....

....

....

....

2. FAITH THAT DOESN'T SAVE (3:2–7)

Rejoicing in the Lord is impossible if we trust in anything besides Christ for salvation. That's what Paul wants us to see next, and in verses 2–7 he identifies a particular kind of misplaced trust. Those who promote this wrong trust Paul calls *mutilators of the flesh* (v. 2). The mutilation he has in mind here is circumcision, which we first encountered in last week's lesson. In the Old Testament, Jewish men were circumcised as a way of indicating their belonging to God's people, and then their sons were circumcised too when they were eight days old. In Paul's day, some of the Jews who had come to believe in Jesus didn't fully understand the gospel. These Jews, called Judaizers, insisted that trusting in Jesus alone for salvation wasn't sufficient. They claimed that in order to really be saved, non-Jewish believers basically had to become Jews, which meant receiving this Old Testament mark of God's covenant, circumcision.

✦ How does Paul describe these Judaizers in verse 2?

In verse 3 Paul explains why the Judaizers are way off base. When Jesus came, he ushered in a brand-new covenant that enables all people, not just Jews, to be grafted into God's family, and the old-covenant requirement of circumcision was no longer necessary. That's why Paul says that Christians are now the true circumcision—because, in Christ, spiritual hearts, not physical body parts, are circumcised.

✦ In verse 3, what three activities characterize the people whom Paul calls "the circumcision"?

The necessity of Paul's harsh words about the Judaizers makes sense when we understand why he says that true believers "put no confidence in the flesh" (v. 3). By saying that circumcision was necessary to become a Christian, the Judaizers were basically saying *Christ + circumcision = salvation*. In other words, they were putting confidence in the flesh—in something they do. The gospel says *Christ alone = salvation*. We contribute nothing to our salvation—not even our faith. Even faith is a gift, something God gives to us in order that we will believe and put our trust in Christ (see Ephesians 2:8–9).

Paul then uses his own life story to illustrate his point about fleshly confidence. He'd been circumcised according to custom. In addition, he'd descended from the Old Testament tribe of Benjamin. This was the tribe that had given Israel its very first king centuries earlier. Paul had also been a proud Pharisee before coming to Christ. Pharisees were Jewish religious leaders who prided themselves on keeping God's laws, and they invented all kinds of nitpicky religious rules. Paul had been one of those leaders—and, in fact, he'd been so passionate about rule-keeping as the way to salvation that he'd persecuted people who trusted in Christ alone for salvation. So Paul had been part of the Jewish elite, a religious bigwig, and he had taken great pride in his heritage. But all that changed in an instant.

✦ Read Acts 9:1–19, which tells the story of Paul's conversion (back in the day when he went by the name Saul). How does this story help us gain a fuller understanding of how coming to know Christ dealt a blow to Paul's pride?

....

....

....

....

✦ Here in Philippians 3:7, how has Paul's view of his prestigious background changed?

....

....

....

....

3. GOOD RIDDANCE! (3:8-11)

So Paul's prestigious background counts for nothing—it can't save him. When it comes to being right with God, all those so-called religious privileges were actually worthless. But that's not all.

✦ According to verse 8, what else besides his religious background has dramatically diminished for Paul, and why?

✦ The zeal Paul had for Christ wasn't because he was some sort of super-spiritual giant. How do Jesus's words in Matthew 16:24–26 show that Paul-like zeal is meant for all of us?

When Paul expresses a desire to "gain Christ" (v. 8), he certainly doesn't mean that he has to strive for his salvation. Because of his union with Christ, his eternal security is guaranteed. Paul is talking about experiencing all the riches of this union. He wants to know Christ in the deepest way possible.

✦ How do the following passages shed light on the way in which Paul desires to *know* Christ, as he expresses it in verses 8–10?

· Jeremiah 9:23–24

What do you live for, Ananias?

Now there was a disciple at Damascus named Ananias. The Lord said to him in a vision, "Ananias." And he said, "Here I am, Lord." And the Lord said to him, "Rise and go to the street called Straight, and at the house of Judas look for a man of Tarsus named Saul, for behold, he is praying, and he has seen in a vision a man named Ananias come in and lay his hands on him so that he might regain his sight." But Ananias answered, "Lord, I have heard from many about this man, how much evil he has done to your saints at Jerusalem." . . . But the Lord said to him, "Go, for he is a chosen instrument of mine to carry my name before the Gentiles and kings and the children of Israel. . . . So Ananias departed and entered the house. And laying his hands on him he said, "Brother Saul, the Lord Jesus who appeared to you on the road by which you came has sent me so that you may regain your sight and be filled with the Holy Spirit."
(Acts 9:10–13, 15–17)

· Ephesians 1:16–19

· Hebrews 8:10–11

· 2 Peter 1:2–3

....

....

....

✦ Paul does a good job in verse 9 showing how believers are made right with God. Summarize what he says.

....

....

....

....

So eager is Paul to know Christ and be identified with him that he sees even his suffering for the sake of the gospel as a part of that (v. 11). And it's important to stress again, as we end our study of this portion of the letter, that Paul is not questioning whether he'll actually make it to heaven. Expressing his hope of laying hold of eternal life "by any means possible" is simply his way of emphasizing his complete dependence on Christ for salvation. No matter how much he pursues the Lord, no matter how successful his ministry, and even no matter how much he suffers for Jesus's sake, nothing he does will earn him a way into heaven. It is Jesus Christ all the way.

LET'S TALK

1. When we read about Paul's passionate zeal for Christ, it's easy to think that he was some unique spiritual giant. We don't often talk the way Paul did or hear others voice such a strong commitment, and, truth be told, we wonder if we'll ever have zeal like Paul's. But because we're in Christ, we are just as qualified, just as able, to live like he did. Discuss how you can cultivate passion for Christ in practical ways. For another hint to what fueled Paul's passion, read 2 Corinthians 5:13–15 as you begin your discussion.

....

....

....

....

....

....

....

....

2. Paul was perfectly okay to let go of everything that hindered him from knowing Christ more fully. Discuss how your own life has changed through becoming a committed follower of Jesus. Consider relationships gained or lost as well as personal interests, desires, places, and pursuits.

....

....

....

....

....

....

....

ONWARD AND UPWARD

PHILIPPIANS 3:12-4:1

How did I get here? We sometimes wonder how we got where we are, usually during a difficult season with no end in sight. During those difficult times, we might do a mental scan through our past, remembering what used to be, and then fantasizing the *what-ifs*: "What if I'd married *that* man rather than *this* one?" "What if I had waited rather than acting on impulse?" "What if I'd reached out for help when I was tempted?" The what-ifs are fruitless because we can't change the past; there's no "undo" key for life. And the what-ifs for each life are unique. For Paul, it was all the years he wasted believing he could earn his way to heaven. Yet he didn't linger there. He didn't waste more time lamenting those lost years. Instead, having discovered that Christ is everything—his life, his salvation, and his joy—he fixed his gaze forward. He wanted to live his life in Christ to the fullest extent possible. That's exactly where Paul takes us next, to the need to apply ourselves to Christian growth. Maturing as disciples requires diligent effort on our part. As Paul wrote earlier in the letter, "Work out your own salvation with fear and trembling, for it is God who works in you, both to will and to work for his good pleasure" (2:12–13). Now, at this point, Paul focuses on how we *work out* what God *works in*, and he shows from his own life and outlook what this pursuit of godliness looks like.

1. LIVING FORWARD (3:12-16)

In last week's lesson, Paul set out a ledger of sorts, with his gains in one column and his losses in another. He wanted to make the point that his losses were nothing in comparison to what he'd gained. This gain is something Paul wants to enjoy to the fullest. Not just later in heaven but now, during his lifetime, he wants to do all he can to experience the riches of his salvation in ever deeper ways.

✦ How does Paul describe his effort in verses 12–14, and what motivates him to make that effort?

....

....

....

....

The trajectory of the Christian life is meant to be forward. Paul makes that point here with his determination to direct his gaze away from the past. When Paul talks about forgetting what lies behind him, most likely he isn't thinking at this point of his pre-Christian life—either the sins he committed or the shallow, superficial things that he'd formerly relied on for right standing with God. He's moved along to focus now on spiritual growth. So in that context, Paul is saying that yesterday's progress is all fine and good, but it doesn't help with going forward today. In other words, Christians—including Paul himself—can't look back on last year's spiritual progress, or even last week's, and use that as an excuse to take a break from the pursuit of holiness. How true it is that we are at all times either going forward in the Christian life or going backward! There's simply no neutral, no coasting. If we think there is, we're going to wind up in spiritual trouble.

> *"Perhaps there is something that God has been asking you to lay aside in order that you might be a more effective witness for him. . . . Will you cast it aside to follow Jesus? If you do, you will grow in your Christian discipleship, and God will bring great blessing into your life and through you also into the lives of others."*[17]

> *"If you really want to know God's will, you must be willing to do his will even before you know what it is."*[18]

✦ How does Paul link spiritual maturity to our thought life in verse 15?

✦ No one becomes spiritually mature apart from God's work, which is why we see again this dual action of believers working out in their lives what God works into their hearts. What does Paul add in verse 15 to our understanding of how this happens?

✦ How do you think we can carry out Paul's charge in verse 16? Consider these verses in your answer: Psalm 25:9; Proverbs 4:23; John 8:31–32; 14:23.

2. MINDS MADE NEW (3:17-19)

Paul has touched on the role of our thoughts in spiritual growth, and he builds more on that idea here by telling us where to focus.

✦ Paul gives two directives in verse 17, both of which involve imitation. In the first one, Paul encourages his friends to imitate him. This isn't the only time Paul urges believers to follow in his footsteps, and he'll even do it again later in this letter. For each passage below, identify the reason given for imitating Paul and, if it's noted, what is to be imitated and how.

	Imitating Paul: Why, What, How?
1 Corinthians 4:15-16	
1 Corinthians 11:1	
Philippians 4:9	
1 Thessalonians 1:6-7	
2 Thessalonians 3:7-9	

In contrast to the godly example of Paul and the other apostles are people whose example must be avoided at all costs. These "enemies of the cross of Christ" are doomed for destruction (3:18–19).

✤ Paul says that the god of these evildoers is "their belly" (3:19). What do you think he means? You might want to look up Romans 16:17–18 and 1 John 2:15–16 to help you answer.

....

....

....

....

✤ The overall thought life of flourishing, mature believers is radically different from the thought life of these "enemies of the cross" (3:18). According to 3:19, how does it differ?

....

....

....

....

✤ We can't help but notice in this letter the priority Paul places on the mind of Christians. And all through the Bible we are told to take charge of our thoughts because what we think about and focus on significantly impacts our lives in ways big and small. We're going to see more about this later in Philippians, but for now, how do passages from elsewhere in the Bible deepen our awareness of this principle?

   · Isaiah 26:3

....

....

....

· Proverbs 28:26

· Romans 8:5–7

· Colossians 3:1–2

3. DESTINED FOR GLORY (3:20-4:1)

Earlier in the letter, Paul encouraged the Philippians to see themselves not so much as Roman citizens as citizens of God's kingdom (1:27–28). He reinforces that identity here and then shows them why citizenship in God's kingdom is so much better than anything offered by the kingdoms of this world.

✦ What does Paul identify in verses 20–21 as the final outcome of our union with Christ?

What do you live for, Epaphroditus?

I have thought it necessary to send to you Epaphroditus my brother and fellow worker and fellow soldier, and your messenger and minister to my need, for he has been longing for you all and has been distressed because you heard that he was ill. . . . So receive him in the Lord with all joy, and honor such men, for he nearly died for the work of Christ, risking his life to complete what was lacking in your service to me.
(Philippians 2:25-26, 29-30)

✦ One day Jesus will return from heaven to gather his people, and that's when the final outcome of our salvation will be completed. Here in verses 20–21 Paul attributes that final outcome to Jesus Christ, the second person of the Trinity, but actually all three persons—Father, Son, and Holy Spirit—are involved in every aspect of our salvation from beginning to end. When it comes to this final outcome, what do we learn in Romans 8:26–30 about the roles of the Father and the Spirit?

✦ In another one of his letters, Paul gives more details of our final transformation. What do we learn about it in 1 Corinthians 15:35–44, 50–53?

✦ Back to Philippians 3, what else do we learn about Jesus Christ in verse 21?

✦ "Therefore"—when we see this word in the Bible, we always need to ask, "What is the 'therefore' there for?" In this case, in the first verse of chapter 4, the word leads us to a conclusion—a practical application—of what Paul has just been saying about our destiny. What is his application in 4:1?

LET'S TALK

1. Is there some aspect of your past—a choice you made, a lifestyle you adopted—that you regret now? If so, talk about how Paul's outlook can help you be free of that. Discuss some practical ways to forget what lies behind and instead to strain for what lies ahead (3:13). Don't come up with general principles; make it personal. How can *you* strain forward in such a way that you are able to leave the past behind?

2. Paul gives clear instructions in 3:17 that we are to keep our eyes on godly people. Discuss whose walk you watch and seek to imitate, and explain what about this person's faith attracts you.

CAN'T WE ALL JUST GET ALONG?

PHILIPPIANS 4:2-9

Maybe you remember the children's nursery rhyme about church that's illustrated with hand gestures:

> Here's the church,
> Here's the steeple;
> Open the doors
> And see all the people.

It conveys a nice, warm feeling about God's gathered people, doesn't it? But the reality of those gatherings is often far different. What disrupts that warmth is "all the people." There's conflict, and it's in every church because the church is made up of sinners like you and me. That's why all through the letter Paul has been stressing the need for unity and, of course, for the servant-hearted humility that makes unity possible. So, finally, as he nears the end of the letter, Paul identifies a particular conflict in the church at Philippi and names the two women at the heart of it. After that, he gives more practical instruction that will help his friends work out their difficulties and continue along the path of spiritual maturity.

1. A TALE OF TWO WOMEN (4:2-3)

Two women in the church at Philippi, Euodia and Syntyche, are not getting along, and Paul directs his next words to this unfortunate situation.

✢ Paul is careful to phrase his plea about Euodia and Syntyche so that it's equally applied to both women. What does he urge them to do? Take a look back at 2:1–2 to more fully form your answer.

_____

_____

_____

_____

In order to bring about reconciliation, Paul turns to another member of the church, an unnamed "true companion," for aid. And then he reminds his readers, first, that the two women had served together in the past, and then, second, that they all share a common destiny—their names recorded in "the book of life" (v. 2).

✢ Paul never identifies the specific conflict, the reason why Euodia and Syntyche aren't getting along. What can this—and the rest of what Paul writes in verses 2–3—teach us about how to work toward conflict resolution in our own fellowship?

_____

_____

_____

_____

2. REJOICE, PRAY, THINK (4:4-9)

Paul seems to steer the subject away from church conflict in verses 4–9, but these verses actually do connect to his plea concerning Euodia and Syntyche. If believers follow the instruction Paul gives in these verses, they are much less likely to experience such conflicts.

✦ The instruction in verse 4 is something we've seen before—"Rejoice." Why do you think Paul might have included this instruction right here, after his appeal to Euodia and Syntyche?

....

....

....

....

✦ Joy is the Spirit-given state of happy security in Christ, whereas rejoicing is active— it's something we actually do. How do the following passages model what rejoicing looks like?

· Ephesians 5:18–21

....

....

....

· Colossians 3:16–17

....

....

....

· 1 Thessalonians 5:15–22

....

....

....

Everything Paul writes in this section is layered, one instruction atop the next. Unity is strengthened through rejoicing, and to rejoicing is added "reasonableness," or gentleness, in verse 5. We can best understand Paul's meaning here when we consider the call to unity and humble, sacrificial love that permeates the entire letter.

✦ In the chart below, note what you learn about the gentleness of the Lord as well as what the Bible teaches about how Christians are to be gentle.

The Lord's Gentleness	Christian Gentleness
Psalm 18:31–35	Proverbs 15:4
Isaiah 40:10–11	Ephesians 4:1–2
Matthew 11:28–30	2 Timothy 2:24–26
Philippians 2:5–7	James 3:16–18

✤ How does that brief overview help us understand why gentleness is vital for unity?

_____

_____

_____

_____

Reasonableness, or gentleness, builds unity. Therefore, as God's people, it's safe for us to deal gently with others, including those with whom we disagree—and who maybe even do us harm—because "the Lord is at hand" (v. 5).

✤ The Lord's nearness—his protective, loving presence with his people—means we can go to him with our relational struggles and with struggles of all kinds. How does Paul guide us in verse 6 about *how* to pray and about *what* to pray for?

· How to pray:

_____

_____

_____

· What to pray for:

_____

_____

_____

✤ What promise does Paul attach to prayer in verse 7, and how is this promise meant to affect us?

_____

_____

....

....

✤ We get a wealth of information about prayer in just two verses here (vv. 6–7). First, we learn that nothing is off limits. We can take all our requests to God, confident that he will hear. We might not get the answer we hope for, but we get something even better. What does Romans 8:26–27, 31–34 reveal as God's most precious gift, whether or not we get the specific things we pray for?

....

....

....

....

Paul begins to wrap up this section by returning to a by-now familiar theme in this letter—our thought life. In verse 8 he lists a number of qualities that can guide us about what to take into our minds (and subsequently our hearts). What's so interesting about this list is that the qualities he names—the Greek words he uses—were not specifically Christian virtues. The words he uses apply to good of all kinds. So Paul is saying that when we make decisions about what to allow into our minds, we are to choose what's pure, lovely, commendable, excellent, and praiseworthy—whatever the source might be. So, for example, reading a classic novel written by a non-Christian might be much more profitable than reading a poorly written Christian romance. The point is that just because something is labeled "Christian" or "evangelical" doesn't mean it's worthwhile. Paul calls us to be discerning.

✤ How might minds shaped by excellent and praiseworthy things foster not only unity but also spiritual maturity? Look also at Romans 12:2 and Ephesians 5:8–10, 15–16 to help you answer.

....

....

....

In verse 9 Paul again encourages the Philippians to imitate him, not only in thought and belief but also in practice—what they do in living out their faith in day-to-day life. And he promises that as they do, God will be with them. He's certainly not saying that their eternal security is on shaky ground! As Paul made so clear earlier in the letter, believers are safe in God's keeping through their union with Christ. Paul's point here is that while our eternal security isn't dependent on our performance, our enjoyment of God's fellowship is. And it would be good to add here that those who have no interest in imitating Paul and other godly examples, and therefore care little about growing up spiritually, are wise to question whether they've ever really known the Lord at all. But Paul doesn't intend to end this section with a somber warning. He's offering encouragement to brothers and sisters whom he knows are pursuing the Lord wholeheartedly. Ups and downs there may be, but they are growing day by day.

What do you live for, Mary of Bethany?

Jesus entered a village. And a woman named Martha welcomed him into her house. And she had a sister called Mary, who sat at the Lord's feet and listened to his teaching. But Martha was distracted with much serving. And she went up to him and said, "Lord, do you not care that my sister has left me to serve alone? Tell her then to help me." But the Lord answered her, "Martha, Martha, you are anxious and troubled about many things, but one thing is necessary. Mary has chosen the good portion, which will not be taken away from her."
(Luke 10:38–42)

LET'S TALK

1. We aren't told why Euodia and Syntyche were disagreeing. Most likely it had something to do with the goings on at the Philippian church, since Paul mentions the controversy in this public letter. Had it been a matter between just the two of them, something that didn't impact the church as a whole, most likely it would have been handled privately. Whatever it was, these two sisters in Christ weren't getting along. Maybe they found

themselves competing to use their spiritual gifts, or perhaps, like Mary and Martha in Jesus's day, one felt she was doing more than her share of the work (Luke 10:38–42). Open up about a struggle you experienced with a Christian sister and how it was resolved. Talk about the impact that the conflict—and its resolution—had on both of you and on others as well. Mention what helped you and also what didn't.

....

....

....

....

....

....

....

2. Some of us choose which movies to view based on the Motion Picture Association film rating system. It actually takes more discernment to apply Philippians 4:8 as a grid for our entertainment choices. How might basing your choices on this verse change what you choose to read, watch, and hear?

....

....

....

....

....

....

....

THE GOD WHO PROVIDES

PHILIPPIANS 4:10-23

Let's admit it—we all like to be let in on a good secret. Some secrets are secretive because someone has something to hide, something that would bring shame and trouble if uncovered. Other secrets are secretive simply because no one has yet uncovered what's just waiting to be found. Paul had a secret, and his was one of those in the yet-to-be-uncovered category. It's a mystery he'd discovered firsthand and now wants to share with his friends. It's a good secret, something to spread far and wide, and we're let in on it this week. We're also going to see why Paul is very grateful for the kindness of his Christian brothers and sisters in Philippi. They, in turn, are grateful to Paul for his ministry among them, a ministry that had begun when Paul established the Philippian church years before. Ever since, the Philippians had supported Paul as he'd taken the gospel message far and wide. The Philippians had lost touch with Paul on occasion, and there were some rough financial times when they weren't able to send monetary support. But when Paul's friends in Philippi learned that he was imprisoned in Rome, they took up an offering and delivered it to Paul in the hands of one of their members, Epaphroditus. That's the reason for Paul's outpouring of gratitude as we draw near to the end of the letter. At the same time, Paul wants them to know that his affection and care—his very ministry—aren't based on financial gifts.

1. THE SECRET OF CONTENTMENT (4:10-13)

More rejoicing from Paul, this time in gratitude for the helpful gift the Philippians have been able to send him. At the same time, he's quick to reassure them that he'll be okay with or without their financial support; in other words, he's contented to live in whatever situation God places him. Contentment isn't automatic, which Paul makes clear in this passage. In fact, as we see, it's something that has to be *learned*. That's why, when we pray for contentment, God rarely answers by simply flooding our hearts with a sense of well-being.

✦ As we consider Paul's contentment, we remember that he's writing about it from a prison cell! And this is not the first time he's suffered for his faith. Read 2 Corinthians 11:24–28. How would you summarize his ministry experience?

....

....

....

....

✦ At one point during his ministry, Paul was given a special revelation from God, a secret glimpse into paradise. So privileged was Paul to be given this vision that he was in danger of becoming conceited as a result. So the Lord humbled him with suffering, what Paul calls a "thorn" in his flesh (2 Corinthians 12:7). Learn about this experience by reading 2 Corinthians 12:7–10.

· How in 2 Corinthians 12:8 did Paul first handle this thorn?

....

....

....

· Paul found the secret of contentment in this situation because of how the Lord answered his prayer in 2 Corinthians 12:9. What is that secret?

....

....

....

> *"Many Christians do not know the joy that
> could be theirs because their lives are not holy
> or they do not trust God for their future."*[19]

· How does Paul summarize this secret in Philippians 4:13?

2. GIVING AS FRUIT AND FRAGRANCE (4:14-20)

Paul is contented with or without the financial aid of his Philippian friends, yet he is, of course, delighted to receive it.

✤ Paul recalls the early days of his ministry, when he came to Macedonia, a region that included the city of Philippi, to bring the gospel message and establish churches. What do we learn about the Philippian church in verse 15?

✤ In verse 16 Paul glances back to his time in Thessalonica, where he traveled for ministry after establishing the church in Philippi. Thessalonica was 94 miles from Philippi. Read Acts 17:1–9, which recounts this visit. The visit came to an end when an angry mob stirred up trouble for Paul and his ministry partners. What do we learn in Acts 17:1–9 about the impact of the gospel and the apostles' ministry at this point?

✦ Paul writes about "fruit" in Philippians 4:17 in the context of giving, telling the Philippians that their gifts to him are ultimately for *their* own spiritual benefit. How does 2 Corinthians 9:6–12 help us understand the nature of this "fruit"?

Glory

The word *glory*, which comes from a Hebrew term that means "heavy" or "weighty," is linked to God all through the Bible. It indicates his power and unmatched majesty, his righteousness and holiness and splendor. "The object of the church is to see that the world acknowledges the glory which is God's (Romans 15:9) and is shown in his deeds (Acts 4:21), in his disciples (1 Corinthians 6:20), and above all in his Son, the Lord of glory (Romans 16:27)."[20]

✦ We learn in verse 18 that the Philippians' latest gift to Paul has been a "sacrifice," which implies that they didn't just send Paul a bit of extra money they had lying around. A sacrifice by definition is something costly, and when we give in this way, God is pleased. We see this also in Hebrews 13:16: "Do not neglect to do good and to share what you have, for such sacrifices are pleasing to God." Here in Philippians 4:18 Paul calls these sacrifices "a fragrant offering," which is how Old Testament sacrifices were described when they pleased God. How does Philippians 2:4–8 help us understand why God is pleased with our sacrifices?

✦ Paul wraps up this section on giving with a tremendous promise in verse 19: "My God will supply every need of yours according to his riches in glory in Christ Jesus." It's important that we see this promise in the context of Paul's big-picture theme here in this section of the letter. If we miss the big picture, we're likely to get a wrong idea of how God fulfills this promise. Look over verses 10–19 and then identify the context—the theme—of this passage. You might also want to take a look at 2 Corinthians 9:8.

Paul ends the body of the letter in verse 20 with what's called a "doxology," which is an expression of praise. In light of everything Paul has written to his Philippian friends—encouragement, exhortation, spiritual instruction, and joy, joy, joy—the only fitting conclusion is to ascribe it all to God the Father: "To our God and Father be glory forever and ever."

3. GOODBYE FOR NOW (4:21-23)

Everyone matters. There are no insignificant church members, which is why Paul and the believers with him send greetings to every single person in the Philippian church.

✦ Again here, as at the very beginning of the letter, Paul calls believers "saints," which basically means "holy ones." Do you find yourself a bit uncomfortable applying this term to yourself and to other Christians you know? If so, how do the following passages help you understand why "saints" is a good way to describe God's people.

   · Ephesians 1:3–4

· Titus 3:4–7

What do you live for, Euodia and Syntyche?

These women . . . have labored side by side with me [Paul] in the gospel together with Clement and the rest of my fellow workers, whose names are in the book of life.
(Philippians 4:3)

· 1 Peter 2:9–10

We might be tempted to skip right over Paul's closing remarks since they're directed to a bunch of people we won't ever know in this lifetime. But there's actually something significant here: greetings from Caesar's household. If there are saints in Caesar's house, it means that the gospel is penetrating the upper echelons of Rome, even if the particular saints Paul writes of here aren't Roman royalty but servants and slaves. The point is, the gospel is spreading in this most unlikely place—the house of the highest Roman official!—and no doubt this news impacted the Philippians, who loved their status as Roman citizens.

Paul ends the letter just as he began—holding out grace, specifically here from Jesus Christ. No more perfect ending could be written: "The grace of the Lord Jesus Christ be with your spirit" (v. 23).

LET'S TALK

1. Would you describe yourself as a contented woman? If not, what seems to be lacking? Discuss Paul's "secret" to contentment and some ways that you can make it your very own.

....

....

....

....

....

....

2. One of the most frequently quoted Bible verses appears in this week's lesson: "My God will supply every need of yours according to his riches in glory in Christ Jesus" (v. 19). We've learned that Paul had something specific in mind with this promise—giving. God wants us to be generous, and he promises to take care of us as we give generously. Does grasping the context of Paul's words change your thinking about how to apply this verse to your life? Discuss how you'll seek to apply verse 19 as Paul intended—as confidence for giving generously.

....

....

....

....

....

....

....

3. What do *you* live for?

4. As we end our study of Philippians, summarize what you have learned about:

· The big story of the whole Bible:

· The character of Almighty God:

· Salvation in Jesus Christ:

HELPFUL RESOURCES FOR STUDYING PHILIPPIANS

Boice, James Montgomery. *Philippians: An Expositional Commentary*. Grand Rapids, MI: Baker, 1971; 2000.

Guthrie, Nancy. "Philippians: John Piper on Philippians," Parts 1 and 2. *Help Me Teach the Bible* podcast. May 21, 2015, https://www.thegospelcoalition.org/podcasts/help-me-teach-the-bible/john-piper-on-philippians-part-1/.

Thielman, Frank. *Philippians*. NIV Application Commentary. Grand Rapids, MI: Zondervan, 1995.